WITHDRAWN
IOWA STATE UNIVERSITY
LIBRARY

D0586330

the

Animal

Inside

poems by Josephine Jacobsen

ohio university press (athens, ohio

the
Animal
Inside

WITHDRAWN
IOWA STATE UNIVERSITY
LIBRARY

Copyright © 1953, 1955, 1956, 1957, 1958, 1959, 1960, 1961,
1962, 1963, 1964, 1965, 1966 by Josephine Jacobsen
Library of Congress Catalogue Card Number: 66–11299
Manufactured in the United States of America by
H. Wolff, New York
Designed by JoAnn Randel

PS3519
A424
A8
1966

for Martha and Erlend, Ricky, Evan and Hilse

with love

868563

Never look unless you
    are prepared to see
everything or
    nothing. . . .

Elliott Coleman
Mockingbirds At Fort McHenry

Acknowledgments

Acknowledgment is made to the following, in which some of the poems in this volume originally appeared: *Commonweal, Beloit Poetry Journal, Contemporary Poetry, Dartmouth Quarterly, Epoch, Herald Tribune, Imagi, Midwest Review, Nation, New Poems by American Poets* (I, II), *New Republic, New York Times, Poetry Awards for 1955, 1958, 1960, 1961, Saturady Review, Voices.*

"The Murmurers," "Water," "The Sea Fog" appeared originally in *The New Yorker.*

"The Revolutionary," "Reindeer and Engine," "The Three Children," "Homage to Henri Christophe," "Mr. Tantripp's Day," "Time Exposure," "Poems for My Cousin," "The Animal Inside the Animal" appeared originally in *Poetry: A Magazine of Verse.*

"The Enemy of the Herds, the Lion" appeared originally in *Poetry Northwest.*

"All Hallows Party" and "Shibboleth" appeared originally in *Prairie Schooner.*

A number of these poems have been recorded by Lee Anderson for the Yale University Collection of American Poets.

Contents

3 POEMS

SEQUENCES

1

. . . *If an animal lives and moves, it can only be, he (the savage) thinks, because there is a little animal inside which moves it; if a man lives and moves, it can only be because he has a little man or animal inside who moves him. The animal inside the animal, the man inside the man, is the soul* . . .

. . . *to this some of the blacks replied, Yes, yes. We also are two, we also have a little body within the breast.* . . .

The Golden Bough

THE ANIMAL INSIDE

The animal inside the animal
is motionless or moves. At midnight, paces.
Almost is ambushed in the mirror.

When his eyes open inward—not to see
but for your sight—its glimpsed shadow is beautiful, dangerous

only to this companion whose it is.
Seen, it can be loved. But how
it is terrible inside the breast.

Here it cannot be caught
to kill or free or tame.
It turns, and goes, and turns,

but rarely, at odd times.
Most often it is still;
as if asleep, or listening.

II. SHADOW-NOTE

There is this footnote to the shadow:
It has the cruelty of innocence.
It will neither make excuses nor give details,
As: this is how it happened . . .
Or: how worn his face was . . .

So that the particular body throws
The universal shadow on the sand,
Carpet, pine-needles, cement, grave-sod—
Telling one thing: the truth
Without proportion, by its mass.

Where the substance would reach the doubtful senses,
The shadow goes past, immediate and in depth,
To your most private recognition
Of a gallows on gravel,
A cat on bright grass.

III. SHADOW IMAGE

The short shadow
Squat and flat
Dwarfs the bole, says short is true;
The tall shadow
Says giant, giant.
But the tree lifts, says green on bluest.

On the black rainbow
Of wet sand
Flies over fast and tilted wing:
The gull's shadow.
And the hand
Casts on the dust its shadow-fingers.

The dark soul
Is shadow-word
Of the beast or man, the dark map
Of its soul, the shade of the bird
For which they set a shadow-trap.

IV. SHADOW WATER IMAGE

The houses waver in the water, waver,
flow over, stain and shudder.

Distorted, faithful, nothing is ignored,
all—contour, color—paired;

all—color, contour—changed. Untouchable:
water is brick and gable.

. . .

If the midnight heart, hunting love's face
meets in its place

his own, now will he drown, by such a loss,
in the silent brightness.

. . .

Narcissus, ravished, leaned a long moment
over this element:

the water-image then with a light shiver
drew down its lover

letting the fountain-laughter play its gleam
over the rooted bloom.

FIRE DATA

I

Disjointed fire forked about the hour:
Old women's ashes rode the wind like kites;
Physicians cauterized the living wound;
The Dump was cleansed by fire, the rats retreated.
And Joan, twisted like paper, flaming up cried "Jesu . . ."

II

These are the tongues of flame from the need-fires.

In the night of Walpurgis, in the eve of Allhallows
To the tame fire come the wild ghosts.

The wolves feared it. (But they waited.)
Later, on the hearth
it imitated love.
Oh the good heat upon the loins and breast.

Come, from the fen, the moor, the leafy place,
revisit the fire you thought tame.
Come cold hand, frosty feet, chill heart,
to your tame flame.

Come, to the gate (it leaps on snow)
the window (it lives shining on the logs)
the door: *It cannot warm you, then.*

These are the tongues of flame from the tein-eigin.

III

These are the tongues of flame from the need-fires.

The green wolf and the leaf king burned,
and the live things inside the osier basket
burned.

Captive and convict in the Beltane fires
for the festival shone, brightly for Baal
burned.

On St. John's Eve, the fire no flint
kindled, fire from the oak
burned.

Before the winter Son, at the sun's lag
at Yule on stone the Christbrand
burned.

Fire on the paschal mountain
in Westphalia for Easter and no easter
burned.

This fire was new. Tongues of the tein-eigin.

IV

The warlock died in fire. Gave up no ghost,
having none to give, but gave a life, cold
as reptile, pride, or tundra:

in the blood's heat, the heart's charity,
the hot hope of heaven, died the warlock,
shredding like chilly sawdust.

His cousin came, cold, cold, astute
as ice at the little center of the heart.
How feed the fire, Christ?

v

The solstice mistletoe, gold bough,
fire's seed, lit the oak: seed
of the sun. Untouchable, you touch
us, tein-eigin of our need.

Descartes, opening his eyes, perceived the visitation
of Grace in a multitude of sparks
of fire about the room: the motion
of dateless fire, in different darks.

From each earth-corner windy fire sprang
The word of flame rushed forking in that wind,
Fell on them native in fiery tongue:
The upper room contained the word's whirlwind.

Hung before the Host, the word of fire
into scatheless flesh burned like hope.
The innocent work of the bees consumes
silently in the colored cup.

VI

Disjointed fire forked about the hour.
Old women's ashes rode the wind like kites,
Physicians cauterized the living wound;
The dump was cleansed by fire, the rats retreated.
And Joan, twisted like paper, flaming up cried "Jesu . . ."

I. I TOOK MY COUSIN TO
PRETTYBOY DAM

I took my cousin to Prettyboy Dam.
A boxer was swimming for sticks, the ripples
Blew from the left, and beer cans glittered
Under the poison-ivy.

We talked of pelota; and of how the tendrils of vines
Curl opposite ways in the opposite hemispheres.
My cousin was dying. By this I mean
The rate of his disengagement was rapid.

There was a haze of heat, and August boys
Chunked rocks at a bottle that bobbed on the water.
The slow hours enclosed the flight of instants,
Melted the picnic-ice.

Everything he saw differently, and more clearly than I.
The joined dragon-flies, the solid foam of the fall;
The thin haste of the ant at my foot,
And me, as I looked at him.

We were close beside each other, speaking of
Pelota, chaining cigarettes when the matches were gone.
But we saw different things, since one could not say
"Wait . . ."
Nor the other "Come . . ."

II. THE FOUR FACES OF MY COUSIN

My cousin had four faces.

One was the face which grimaced
In laughter or anger—mobile to danger,
Fun or sudden love;

Made up of flaws, joys, private
Recall; of a benediction
Or so, and sudden love;

With the harassed grain, and strains
Of wretched encounters, the thought
Of difficult heaven, and sudden love.

The second, was the blast of agony:
Contorted, it glared without sight
When the sheet was turned from the face

By familiar fingers. It glared
Without rest under the harsh gesture
Of death, and the mouth was frantic for its breath.

The third, silent, and silently watched
By the crucified man, had tiny pulses
Of light on its false tranquility—

The candle's mark. It was a good mask,
Composed to duty and not unbeautiful
Below the poised and frilly inner lid.

But the gray-white was wrong, and the faint rouge
On a dead man's lips—(and the fingers
Curled stiffly, shared the face's error.)

The fourth face of my cousin I have never
Seen. This is the secret accurate intended
Face I must wait for.

III. ARRIVAL OF MY COUSIN

My cousin is arrived in
the green city of the dead.
It slopes, shapes itself
in hilly contours, and the summer light
lights all the white stones, crosses and angels of granite.

Thousands or tens of thousands
in the cool grass, under the flight
of birds, of shadows of birds; the shadow
of flight in the sunny marble,
the bird-notes, bird-calls, dew-clear;
The blue and white sky is bent over my cousin,
in the green city of the dead.

Traffic sweats and stalls on Oliver Street,
and Hargrove, Dolphin, Bethel Streets; the dirty bars
sweat, and the usual accidents in the accident-rooms
are glazed by July, as are the gutters and the junk-man's
horse, jerked up the tar-soft mountain of July.
My cousin, however, is in
the green city of the dead.

Not being of a primitive tribe
I speak in metaphor when I find my cousin,
cloud-free, granite-still, in
the green bird-rich city, bounded
by the sweating streets, and the houses, and rooms,

and the people in streets, houses, rooms,
and their eyes.
By the body of Christ we ate, his absence
is evident:
But I speak of the token, the image
I was given for identity;
that word of flesh, like a name, a sound,
is what I speak of.

Infinitely not of the alley, the gutter, the traffic,
the sweating problem that walks
the pavement, sits in the room—
is the token, the word, the vanishing image of my cousin
under blue sky, white cloud, grass, bird-call, stone angel
in the green city of the dead.

I. HE LIT THE STOVE ON A CLOUDY MORNING

The appalled heart at goosegray dawn,
As pale as ash, as old as lichen,
Goes down the stair in dogged flesh,
Beats coldly faint across the floor.
He takes both through the swinging door
Into the empty early kitchen.

The feather-sky sags on a mountain
Black-masked and eyeless as a mole—
He peers into the stove's round hole,
As chilly as a witch in hovel,
Then sends his diamond-hungry shovel
Into the swart slick shine of coal.

Now the heart kindles under its rib
For up, moon-size, the sun-disc goes
And burns the milky mist to blue
And purifies the dark to wonder.
He warms his hand where pulses under
The stove-lid purgatory's rose.

II. HE BROUGHT THE MORNING PAPER
FROM THE MAILBOX

Like lovers they move to this, like lovers in their trance,
Always toward each other; hot or cold,
Moon, neon, candle, sun; in every weather
That is not yet this weather,
Like lovers the killer and his to-be-killed
Choose, move, maneuver. Like lovers in a dance

Still strangers, ignorantly still, advancing they use
The lesser intimacies: summer, a smashed wave,
Spaghetti instead of clams; an evening of laughter;
Select the kind of laughter;
Are afraid, but not of this. Like lovers, like dancers, they move
By choice, but draw nearer with each motion they choose.

And always while they fumble for change, whistle, sleep
Under each other's moon, choose the polka-dot tie,
The canary sweater, the days like veils dissolve
Fast fast and faster; they descry
Naked and steep the ultimate intimate sight:

The animal struggle, if only in the eyes' pain,
In turn flashes—like dying warlock fought—
Through serpent, fox, dove; to the last pose
The held submissive pose
Of forever. The sudden Escaped, the towering Caught.
They came to this around childhood corners and adolescent
    rain.

III. AND AFTER DUSK THERE WAS A
SHOW OF SLIDES

The three looked, across the room, straight on
The Spanish mountains
Big and wild and dark. Shone
Sunny haycocks; shone at their base
A field of wheat; acres of wheat
And vertical navy miles of mountain.

They breathed great air in that focussed cheat
Of heavenly distance
When hairy darkness sat on wheat
Suddenly. A black and giant fly
Blotted the haycocks and the gold
And set his fly-legs across distance:

Four balanced his hugeness, he briskly whetted
Two; like a toy
Of fear he stopped their breaths, he netted
Their breaths in the evil gauze of his wings
Flung over yellow wheat and cocks
Of hay. Then he moved, like an ugly toy

And reason and faith ran. Down dropped
The stupid breath.
The fragile monster started, stopped,
Pittered over a tiny mile of boulders
And black suddenly into blackness went,
Releasing Spain and screen and breath.

IV. WITH THE ANCIENT DOG,
HE STEPPED OUTSIDE AT MIDNIGHT

With him went the black small beast.
A dark wind shook the tamarisks
But could not blow the stars and moon about.

The dog had always vanished;
Never, once, come back unasked
Till now, tonight, quick as though menaced

By something in the humor
Of signals: the wind's tentative sound,
That watch-and-wait of eyes, stellar and lunar.

For close to the dog was a shape.
By the lit door love stood its ground.
The dog looked up in fear, in habit and hope.

At just this balance, beast and human,
The windy midnight spoke two words
Old and new for them to hear in common

Distinctly: *love* and *death*.
Then they moved, separate, and the door
Shut them inside together, for tonight at least.

And through the smallest hours
The still house like a brittle spar
Rode out the night among the jagged stars.

PERSONAE

Vibrations of snow
pulse past the still boles:
the bare boughs move like a mobile of death.

In a Pennsylvania farmhouse I peer
through Quaker windows at the storm.
Ten thousand minutes ago I was in Haiti.

Cold cold cold. Toussaint in his Alpine cell,
dead, drawn up like a monkey from the cold
that froze the heat of Haiti in his blood.
Dying he spoke of Dessalines the Tiger, and of
     Henri
Christophe somewhere in the Haitian hills.

But they were too far away and it was too cold;
     and his fatigue must
have been enormous.

They were all tired, before the end, in one way
     or another:
Dessaline tired perhaps from hate
as the ash is the flame's fatigue. But then in
     pieces in its bloody sack
his body rested.

Henri Christophe. L'Homme, they called him.
     Vive l'Homme!

Grenada? St. Kitts? On some earth floor he
    thrust
into the shock of breath.   *his birth*

That fortress against nothing. The Citadel. La
    Ferrière:
it rides its mountain, heavy with anger, rank
with pride; its great stone beak evil
prows into the evening green
like a ship. He mortared it with pain—
his own and others'.
He was a mason when he was a child.

    I I
The bats come out at dusk; at dusk
Haiti is always on the edge of something;
it stirs it stirs. The peaked stone shelter
built over the quicklime pit is still, however.

Liberty in his ear was foreign, in his blood
    native;   *his youth*
it ticked in his heart like a bomb.
A man's black young possession, he held
the horse and racked the billiard score.
That bony click on the green felt, he carried
to Sans Souci.
As a king, that is.

He saw so much while that bomb ticked like
    doomsday.   *his youth*

Ogé, and Chavannes, at their torture.
A crowd followed the pitiful heads freed
from the body's wreckage.
Toussaint followed, and Dessalines. He watched,
and racked his score.

When he lay in his satin gown like a player,
with the silver bullet in the breech of his pistol—   *his memories*
(he could hear the first snarl of the crowd,   *on his deathbed*
the great palace—without care indeed—almost
empty, except that his daughters, named like
     players,
were in a room, Athenaire, Amethiste,)
which were the ghosts?   *of the revolt*
Boukman and his bowl of blood hot from the
     boar
in Bois Caiman that night? the oath? blood
     vowed
in blood for blood?

Eight days eight nights, the circuses of blood
and the phoenix-breasted flame.
Dessalines, Toussaint, Christophe.
L'Homme. Vive l'homme!

He lifted the dark land. Fire, blood, sword, fire
but still the force was savage love
that knocked his blood in drumbeats in his ear,
to see the country shine, the green dark country.
He dragged it up the mountain on his back.

When did it change, that oldest serpent-change?
The power in his blood turn toward thick stone?
I saw a giant jungle mahogany, wound
in the arms of figier maudit   *of his pride*
that sprang from a seed in a bird's feces:
thick as a devil, fluid in its hardness,
without a sound and over great time it killed.

Around his bones towers La Ferrière.   *of the ghost*

In the mad melodrama of dream
this is familiar—the hot empty church
you burst into, and knelt in extremity, and lifted
your eyes. There—his head still on his shoulders
      like a lie—
moved the priest-celebrant.

It was the word you waited and you fell.   *of his stroke*

The jewel-goddess girls, the Duke of Lemonade,
the French priest's ghost, the palace and the
      monstrous monument,   *of his haste*
the silver bullet—true fairytales   *and his courage*
to screen us from the black and dying man
who carried a land upon his back
while the bomb ticked too quickly for more
      than hope.

In sober fact, after the fairy bullet one man one
      woman and two girls

fought up the wicked path with that great
body. And this by dark.
The new Haitian sun struck the inner court
like minted metal, and the quicklime,
meant for bricks you understood,
sucked as it took you.
The dead citadel buries its dead.

his burial in
the limepit at
La Ferrière

But all that glory sank to green the forest
stain the great flowers and knit the roots.
There is a circle but it cannot hold you.

Liberty's lover breeds slavery from her flesh
and slavery breeds its parricide.
But the first day stays true.
Somewhere deep in the earth, dissolved in the
      sky like rain,
like rain, goes its own circle. You are free now.

The need for freedom is a desert-thirst.
You had it and you gave it.
This is a strange thing: ambushed by power like
      a fiend, yes, but
this was not the man.
His blood hums in the veins of rivers and
the red sun sheds it back on the rich earth.
Vive l'Homme.

The Quaker storm slants faster.
A mouse is at work
in the cold wall. The night gleams like a shell.

This thing is strange. You cannot spell
liberty. It is whole and avid for air.
Dark land in the blue sea, be free in him.

In the hot sun and dazzle of grass,
The wind of noise is men's voices:

A torrent of tone, a simmer of roar,
And bats crack, bags break, flags follow themselves.

The hawkers sweat and gleam in the wind of noise,
The tools of ignorance crouch and give the sign.

The deaf-mutes sit in the hurricane's eye,
The shell-shape ear and the useless tongue

Present, but the frantic fingers' pounce-and-bite
Is sound received and uttered.

If they blink their lids—then the whole gaudy circle
With its green heart and ritual figures

Is suddenly not: leaving two animal-quick
Wince-eyed things alone; with masses and masses

And masses of rows of seats of men
Who move their lips and listen.

While secret secret sits inside
Each, his deaf-mute; fingerless.

Certainly he knew her face well enough; had studied this
(perhaps this only), under the leafy stars in
the blown mountain midnight, with its sentry
the only waker, except herself and him.

Even by noon (clear as the dazzle
in his cupped palms, or the map he must draw
in red), her identity could scarcely escape him
who had held her on the cold ground asleep or awake.

Though it was by midnight in the hush of hope and silence
of stars that he studied the sleeper best—he, her lover and guide.
His means were sparse, you understand: her face;
his map (in red); his sentry; and a handful of rifles.

After the map of her city broke to glory
(with her there, close, intimate as his blood),
worn with triumph, he fetched up in a proper bed.
Woke in the early sun, at the sound from her

and looked straight into hot whore-eyes that stared
straight into his. He could not fix the moment of change.
So he kept calling her by the old name he had used
for the face he had trusted under the confident stars.

My uncle, a child in the terrible second coming
tottered, too, but no one cried out for pleasure.

In the nursery of the dead his duplication was faithful: toothless
and without words among the wicked toys of enamel
he teetered with one hand raised in the benediction of paralysis.

The caged and simple thing inside him watched
the parts' disintegration.

Through the window's green spaces came
leaf-sound in motion, the scent of roses
traveled, and airborne tigers landed delicately
on their fragile warped globe. The moon
moved at night, staring, and the clouds
approached in silence and turreted softly away. The earth
spun so unobtrusively that the children
receding like a trick picture (only more slowly)
shuffled and lay and never flew into space.

Inside the nursery each thing grew huge: huge spoon
huge bed-crank; the bed-bars barred
Atlantic and Pacific and the hall,
excluding the restless dragon-glitter of the scaly world.

The children, reprimanded, fed, and prattled to,
called often for the famous visitor.
But when he came it was always for someone else.

At night the nursery slept. My uncle,
the bridegroom of another summer, slept, one hand
on his desire, the pinned bell.
On the nights he lay awake, revenants
smiled in the door but never leapt the lintel.

The simple indivisible watcher waited.
It peered forth without warning, using my uncle's eyes
or expressed itself suddenly in a powerful silence closing his lips.
Ninety Julys were there.
What it selected from the offerings no one could tell.

But love (lips to the grill)
shaped its word (in this latest July, in this imperfect hell **never**
    fool-proof,
from which escapes could never be eliminated)
and once, in a quick smile of great sweetness,
my total uncle answered.

Agnes lived with geraniums on the window-sills,
A ginger cat to arch for caresses,
Crisp little bibs on black little dresses
And excellent salads of herbs and cresses;
She was careful with the birthdays of nephews and nieces
     and with Wedgwood and bills.

Agnes' voluble knowledge hobnobbed with psyche and sex:
She knew the causes of early senility
The remotest tribal rites-of-fertility
How the Aztec warriors proved their virility,
And her yellow kitchen was spick, and span was her Celotex.

Agnes knew the thicket where the psychosomatic malingers,
The root that the rat of fear is nibbling
The secret hate of sibling for sibling,
She took her incest without any quibbling
And she blushed to the roots of her hair when the postman
     touched her fingers.

At three o'clock their fingers gripped. The sun shot
a big triangle on his sheeted knees. Their fingers
gripped, after argument, in love. His heart beat quiet
invisible and important. Love, like an inept knife
in her hand, had made lacerations but brought no news.

At nine her fingers gripped a pen; his curved
on air, still warm, but faintly. One man let go
her pulse, invisible, important; the other held
the paper still, so she could write her name, and his
who lay with his mysterious heart stopped.

The hall gave a soft sound like a shore or seashell,
the light was aqueous, too. The black floor shone,
the rubber soles went hushing the white shoes.
His door was closed; the other doors ajar.
She wrote his name so they could find his heart.

When she saw him next he was most formal,
stone hands crossed and a familiar coat
buttoned above the wounds the knife had made.
Their knife was better, it had told them something;
hers had not taught her what she wished to know.

She stole my pencil-case, red leather,
soft, and ten years my friend.
It zipped. Thirty-one pencils in it
long to short, like Aaron's rod
multiplied, held fountains in their spiral.
She was observed: too late I heard;
she sat, sniffled, sniffled, sat, and while I got
white paper out
she stole my case.

While I the ninny peered under chair legs
and slapped my pockets, she vanished like a wolf,
the droop-nosed sniffling gray-green bitch!
A torn kodak: (pony, child, and woman
whose light hand lifted beat off the sun from her eyes,)
was in the case.
Dust sugared the pony's hooves, the woman squinted in that sun
9000 days ago. I carried it with the pencils
and very precious it was. The thief
dropped her handkerchief over the case, dropped
that in her purse and vanished like a wolf—
the sniffling, shuffling, sadistic thief.

Now my pencils are gone—raped from the paper's touch—
Venus, Faber #2 and a yellow Mogul stub, mongrel-sharp,
that had Monte Alban and a tense noon
by those terrible stones, in its yellow shaft.
The Venus had a thing about the Wallendas
and how pyramids go down, or some

at least, and how when the safe hearts vicariously panicked
the clown called for quiet.
But the mongrel would have bayed
at a flight of birds—not the birds, but the flight—
mechanics of feather and current and the eyes' escape.

Now a snuffling wretch with a mean quick thumb has scooped
    it—
my scarlet fetish that held possibility:
the dead July, and the pony's dusty twitch and the woman's
gesture;
and my performing pencils.
Manège horses, incognito,
straining against a mountain of junk in an August alley,
they will lie, in her service—they will limit
the butcher's guile.

She slipped into an elevator, silly, with her prize
and my poems locked in it.

O Dismas do not ask me to be mild—
to the mean gray wretch, the hag,
the pencil thief!

I asked Corrigan about the man, alone at the wood's edge,
Who stood in shadow; the motionless stranger,
He did not stir or speak, and he bore in his face and eyes
The marks perhaps of terrible cold and certainly hunger.

I had come through the journey alive, and into the field
And the sun would have warmed the dead and made them an-
    swer;
And I saw the way he stood, and his coat, and hands.
A stranger returned from this trip is more close than a brother.

So I spoke the word of the way, and he answered once;
But he never moved or came through the windy flowers.
And I said to Corrigan, "He is one of them
But he will not smile or speak—only watches the mowers.

"The field will be gone," I said, "while he stands and looks—
Tell him I am one—though I went, it is true, in summer."
But Corrigan would not question him and the mowers moved
Bright in the glitter of grasses, toward the newcomer.

"Bitter and strange, I agree, in summer as in winter;
But different in winter. Also," Corrigan said,
"Tell me: when you went, and lived, and returned—
Did you travel alone, and without bread?"

Brother Peter Considers Mulroy Drunk under the Rosebush

Let us give praise where praise is due:
the rose sprang single and dew
y; sprang rosy as roses do.

We must announce what we face:
Mulroy lay flat upon his face—
we can see but his surface;

his surface was clogged and lew
d; under the rose rose fern and blue
t, over the rose the wind blew.

This puzzle let us air:
the rose nods on God's air;
Mulroy is Christ's heir.

Poetry to Mulroy's slack p rose,
rose, like the puzzle, g rows—
fragrant, slick-stem, dewy rose.

Mulroy (white, gross and seed
y); bright strong rose, we con cede,
both grew lavish from God's seed.

Clear rose, springing ove
r thick sour flesh, gross g love—
Which is—strange—the be love
d of the Mighty? Strange fierce love.

At Ur
the Lady Shub-ad's small
bright box went into the larger darker
shelter of the grave and stayed there roughly
forty-five hundred years.

Its lid—
a sharp arc—shows a thing:
a lion-sheep without division,
lion on top, sheep under, still
consummation point.

The sheep
neck is in the lion fangs
the lion claws press upward the sheep throat, they are
tranced and ardent in an act of taking
utter enough to be love.

Back so far,
the mind tires on its trip;
so close, the salve, or kohl, to redden
the lip, lengthen the eye for pleasure's
pleasure, is tonight's.

What
is changed? Not the coarse hairs

* *The enemy of the herds, the lion feeds on its prey on decorated box-lid,*
ca.2500 B.C. which was found in the grave of the Lady Shub-ad at Ur.
Magazine of Natural History

of the mane; victor, or victim; a woman's body;
certainly not a death; not the colours
of kohl or scarlet.

She
cared for the box; by wish
expressed or guessed she took it along
as far as might be. Why this one? What
word did her box-beasts mean?

Possi-
bilities: the chic symbols
of the day, on a fashionable jewel-toy,
the owner modishly ignorant; or, corrupt,
an added pulse to lust.

Or:
mocking, or wise, remembrance
of innocent murder innocent death,
the coupled ambiguous desire,
at dinner, at dressing, at music.

Or,
best, and why not? of her meeting
all quiet terror, surmounted by joy,
to go to her grave with her; a pure
mastery older than Ur.

I saw three pairs of eyes which later, at night,
Shone at me baleful as stars.
I could not quench or cloud them. To give them their due
They intended me no ill, but gazed so intently
With their caged and different-colored fires:
They were grape-pulp green, cherry black and survival blue.

Though turned on me, they watched something else:
The green eyes stared inside a small trap
In the shape of a room with the bloom of dust and a stopped
    clock.
With the utmost concentration they watched for the dust to lift
At a breath; like hope embalmed they stared
As if eyes could make a dead clock tick.

Eyes colored to shine like cherries in the leaves,
The black eyes, looked at a façade
Got up with all the claptrap of a mummer:
Balls, sockets, grin, and the swirling hole
Of dark at the center; fixed in the stare
Of the panic force to call back summer.

The blue eyes, clamped to their fiery search
Like the hand's flesh clamped to a blaze of matches,
The lost eyes, flinching but wide, shone
In their fear of finding; minute by minute
By minute, surviving, the blue eyes searched,
Set wide in the enduring unseen bone.

Terrible stars, leveled all at me, they shone
So that I cried to the star-controller, "Keep
Your stars, or change them!" But there was no error
Evidently, for the eyes maintained their regard
Of room, façade, and search. Still and deep
Shining all at me—as if a mirror.

He was naked in water,
the house all quiet, the raw bulb hanging,
when the great June bug
came booming and crashing
thutter and thutter and soft pop deadly
against the raw brilliance.

Outside the night stared like a monster
million-eyed, gold-eyed, over the mountains;
not a clock-tick, a tap-drip, just
that stutter and thunder.

Then hurt and threshing and lying and dying
and silence. So he saw
what had only been known; all alone, and at night:
how light

burns.

Down the wet-leaves steps comes the tiger-head
slowly. Five feminine years timid and proud
move the striped stuff toward joy; the limp tail slips behind.

Follows the smaller skull-capped cautious shape,
fraternal, one-footing after the tufted tail-slip.
The terrace swarms with laborious monsters of the maternal
    mind.

Leaves. Years. Years. Leaves . . . the play will turn more gruff.
There will be treats; and certainly tricks enough.
In some weather she will meet her tiger, his skull will come true.

But they acknowledge that future now and step down, near,
into, the toothy jack-o-lantern light with fear
and courage. Though watched by witches they shall have their
    due.

Hunter, Immobile (45

In another land (or hour) how fierce and cunning
he would be for his celestial rights:

hacking the creepers, swimming cheek by jowl
with crocodiles, staring the tiger down;

crouched under the thin moon, at his trip's end,
till the signal: there-or there. For a hutful of glory,

for a chalice on a suitcase in a loft. For four words
at night, or the least-brave hour before dawn.

But smugness never looked like a wicked river; and the boor,
the lout, the bigot, showed not fangs nor fur.

Scenting small hunger in communion-breakfasts,
he ignored news of any final supper.

And hid his hunter's heart, without a quarry—
forgetful how tigers are sometimes masks and masks are tigers.

Mrs. Throstle said in her garden girdled by meadows and
       mastered by mountains—
       "Here I am close . . ."
by a passion of poppies and white tranced lilac
and the gold-edged breeze-tipped tick
       of the petals' time—
       "This is my altar . . ."
the motion of wings and the costly clash
of dewdrops shivered on poppies on lilacs—
       "Here is my temple . . ."
       said Mrs. Throstle.

Where the injured rat is dispatched by the mongrel
the atheist alleys refract the glitter
       and the garbage witch
       goes jumbling and peering
over the gutters' varied and various offerings
into cans that are sweet with the breath of July,
       the godless garbage of
       poor Mrs. Throstle
where the painful witch goes dying and creaking.

In the cell that rustles at night like a motion
the cell all complete and old with a nation
       that is always one,
       one only, one ever,
no star no sun no messenger moon
but insane time's face that shrinks and swells,

riven from God in her alter egos
      poor Mrs. Throstle
      poor Mrs. Throstle
her deity-decor all lewd and locked.

Yellow

Yellow became alive.
Materialization took place.
First logically with lemons,
then fresh butter.
Also a chair-leg.
After that it appeared
to carve the curve of clouds
and, as sun, shatter them.
The stars grew yellower
yellow whirls on wheels on whirls
leaves flew yellow
the corn sprang
yellow and the crows
winged with a yellow nimbus.
Finally his face
had brilliant yellow
in its grain.
Outside the madhouse hung the yellow sun.

Else has blown away on the east wind, Richard went away with
the wind from the west.
Hilary was taken by the wind from the true north.
Still the south wind is here today but the children are gone. Like
witches or fairytale sons
They came in a three. Like roses or leaves
Or laughter they were gusty. The roses moved and the clear
leaves, the weather was sunny.
The turn is warm today and the leaves limpid and the roses run-
ning.

Else turned somersaults on the granite flags, she had had two
years to learn whatever she had learned.
She loved fear and a great black dog knocked her down
and licked her rumpled face and she screamed for joy. She
waltzed on the steep steps and languished through the ban-
nisters.
Richard had thirteen more months and the plans of monsters
Much on his mind. Richard hoped all things while the tricky
earth turned him over and over.
He was benevolent and wept only at wickedness

And the wind moved his hair and the leaves and roses around
him. Hilary had a secret or two
Too heavy to touch. He dazzled and dawdled
And understood, with reluctance, thorns and chlorophyll **and**
frost in roses and leaves and winds.
He has gone to school to learn simpler things.

The kind gardens of kindergarten have opened their mazes of
    reassurance to Richard and Else.
Here the winds made the summer of leaves and roses

Blow flying and running about them. The black dog bounded, the
    thunder moved and the hours blew round.
On the tomato-sprayer the cross-bones and skull
Behind the pail in the shed smiled at them, but briefly. In the
    peaked house hung the still bell
And the crayon-man figure was pinned
To sticks and the flames like roses blew in a wind's ghost. The
    children in secret wonder
Watched the faces that watched them.

This is one summer not another. Goodbye, three children never to
    be seen again. *We will come back*
They said, but they will not. They will go so quietly, so com-
    pletely.
Next summer three strangers whose names were handed like
    torches from the three that went on the north,
East, west winds, from the three who did not could not stay and
    went forever
At no moment with no gesture, irrecoverable as a single petal or a
    green ghost flying, who went
Where?

Goodbye Else, Richard, Hilary, goodbye, goodbye. Goodbye.

He had a devil's look; and no rain—
The Mexican jungle rain-hungry,
The gods certainly angry,
The Mexican earth in dry pain—
The birds thirsty and the men and the grain.

But even with his mysterious coming, and his skin,
And the drought's brassy eye
The chief said, "Let him say.
If he is not a devil let him begin—"
(Though he has come and with the pallor of sin.)

In the dialect he could not say "Yes," or "No," "Old" or "Young."
But the chiefs waited, even then,
While a runner fetched the men
(Two), who could speak the Outside tongue.
They were reasonable and patient, though the drought had been
     long.

It was Spanish, of course. He could only plead
In English, in German. He cried, not in the Inside
Nor the Outside tongue, in his public need
He gibbered hell's speech.
But a devil can bleed.

* A few years ago, a young German-American painter was the victim of a ritual murder at the hands of some remote Central American Indians, into whose village he strayed alone during a prolonged drought.

Quartered, they carried him, within the rite,
North, South, East, West. The rains
Came promptly to the grains,
The men's, the birds' dry throats.
And flowers sprang like speech, to sight.

POEMS

3

From the ripe silence it exploded silently.
When the bright debris subsided
it was there.

Invisible, inaudible; only
the inky shapes betrayed it.
Betrayed, is the word.

Thence it moved into squalor,
a royal virgin in a brothel,
improbably whole.

It had its followers, pimps, even
its lovers. The man responsible
died, eventually.

When the dust of his brain left the bones
the bond snapped. It escaped to itself.
It no longer answered.

On the shelf, by the clock's tick, in the black
stacks of midnight: it is. A moon
to all its tides.

At night, alone, the animals came and shone.
The darkness whirled but silent shone the animals:
The lion the man the calf the eagle saying
Sanctus which was and is and is to come.

The sleeper watched the people at the waterless wilderness'
    edge;
The wilderness was made of granite, of thorn, of death,
It was the goat which lightened the people praying.
The goat went out with sin on its sunken head.

On the sleeper's midnight and the smaller after hours
From above below elsewhere there shone the animals
Through the circular dark; the cock appeared in light
Crying three times, for tears for tears for tears.

High in the frozen tree the sparrow sat. At three o'clock
The luminous thunder of his fall fractured the earth.
The somber serpent looped its coils to write
In scales the slow snake-music of the red ripe globe.

To the sleeper, alone, the animals came and shone,
The darkness whirled but silent shone the animals.
Just before dawn the dove flew out of the dark
Flying with green in her beak; the dove also had come.

The chinese windchimes
stir
suddenly thin glass rings on thin glass
great leaves
nod
sideways sideways petals stir
to let it pass
clang-cling it plays.

My ribs lift up and
fall
my parted lips could dance a feather
under my palms both
your shoulder-blades fall and
lift
together with that huge light breath.

They are formidable under any feather
and each name; of fly, of sharp sound, soft sound or flower:
oiseau-mouche, zum-zum, beija flor—these on the wing.
Their color? Science cries like a lover, of their light:
Heliomaster, Stellula, Chrysolampsis, Sapphira—sun
fire, star fire, torch fire, jewel fire in the air.

Honey, honey—what rapacity! All the air
vibrates with that passion. Ravage, ravage—wing
and beak and raging hunger plunge them, flower by flower,
along the raceme nodding balanced on the light;
the brief immortelle on its yellow great tree of sun,
hog-plum, ixora, wear like a nimbus their fire and feather.

At night, if they wish, they can die; but not quite. Feather-
light, lax, you may handle them, head limp, wing
elegantly shut. But dive up into blue air
at a moment. In 1653 Father Cobo taught the light
of the Resurrection to the Indians by that power. The sun
on their plumage might have served for the Trinity in flower,

requiring three in one—light, angle, eye, to flower
into their color; lacking one, they go colorless as air.
Interference is the cause of iridescence: feather-
shaft, barb and barbule—must have its sun
as seer; its color is structural, and light
knows this is not a pigment but a murmur of wing.

Water lovers, waterfall lovers, by wet wing
they go, pool shatterers, wet leaf drinkers, light-

ing on nothing; dew drainers, their drenched elected flower
magnetizes metal. Elliptical platelets, feather-
soft? goldsmith stuff inlaid with an eye to air?
Murmurers, feast, fight, flash in the Tobago sun!

Stronger than striped tigers, hotter-blooded, that sun
seethes in their blood; the brilliant obedient air
frees them from patience, fear and commitment. Flower
or hawk they manoeuvre, the murmurers: by wing, by wing
fight, feast, flash—as though the color's feather
on breast, racket tail, gorget, were an attribute of light.

Songless, belligerent, airy bone and feather,
the round sun like a fruit swells to draw your wing
and needle beak, and the whole island's flower is the sound of
    your light.

We met in the city.

Love, if the earth were to my teeth
I would say this, so
listen.
We met in the city.

Who held it, who assaulted, we could not be sure
ever.
Spies passed as children and heroism
mined it like tunnels.
We believed
it had changed hands often—should we fear
besiegers or besieged?
Certainly the peril was extreme.

It was most often night—the bone stones
whitened like echoes of the moon;
the shadows geometric and significant
hid opportunities or only a passerby.
The barbarous birds with cries
like tin torn
swept close; moon and dark
masked the zebra rocks and our own fingers.

For all the patrols and wire, a room blazed
often in a ripped building like a secret
mysterious and blatant: music, voices,
and under the music, laughter.

But the barricades were shifted
constantly and names and addresses were false.

Every so often a dawn
wide solemn and silent, melted the stones
with almost lemon light and absolute stillness. One
lasted for hours once; and once a noon
exploded and folded the night in sun
a dust of summer grass and an image of sheep.

The noon was too circular and told us nothing—
or so we thought at the time.
But the rare dawns altered all angles always
and a map appeared, starry and strange
and familiar and frightening.
I saw it on your body—veins and angles
features and colours the same but different;
after dawn came night and the great birds ripped by.

The three-legged cat paused, cocked her
mouse at us, both zebra-striped;
the hunchbacked tart greeted us gently.
What made us think the city's fall
this time would be
to the final conqueror?

We knew it.

We never failed to find each other.
By luck by love by some grotesque device

can you believe it? in those acres of rubble
those meadows of midnight those moonlight stridencies—
later, or sooner,
bearing new marks or chinking gold like thieves,
under the wings' rush, in the zebra shadows,
we saw the angles, nerves, blood, veins,
glance, gesture,
the shorthand code the message of each other.
O it was worthwhile!

That city.
When moonlight filled it like a cistern
it gave back some reflection—
liquid, moving, distorted—

a chart or map or an equation
in its degenerate wavering glass.

If the earth were to my teeth
I would say
so:
we met in the city.
But we met.

At midnight
it began to rain.

The sound of rain everywhere
fills my hollow ear.
The dry weeks round I was not thinking of that sound—
two sounds, the sound
of falling and the sound of drinking—
now here.

Dusty root darkens and the stubble sharpening
its cruel shafts, softens;
my hollow ear harkening
hears stubble green and moisten,
all drinking all darkening;
the liquid beaded sigh
of sound, two sounds
everywhere and here
in the hollow avid ear.

All need is dry.
Rain is the metaphor.

The eyes of children at the brink of the sea's
Grasp, dilate, fix; their water-sculpted hair
Models their heads; crouching a little they stare
In motionless ecstasy of panic
As the upreared load, tilting, tilting titanic
Pitches and shocks them in a rainbow crash
And is upon them in a cat's flash
Before the nearest shrieks and flees.
Most true terror carries them high to us
Up sand as white and dry as safety—thereafter
Gooseflesh and shudders rack them to drunken laughter,
They reel, self-conscious, pantomiming . . .
But presently sober, cautious down the shining
Dark slope of invitation, outward, to the prize
Of shaping danger they go—and widen their eyes
Innocent and voluptuous.

Never can spring be known so well
As in this wicked dark December,
Nor touched—all emerald and limber—
As in this winter citadel.

The expatriate, in every country,
Encountering alien custom, presses
More closely to the land that graces
His memory, secret, beyond sentry;
The lover in the crowded room
Empty of the one essential,
Creates the missing face, more vital
More fresh than when it touched his own.
So now the death chill at the core
As if the weather struck with fangs,
So now the absence of all wings
Upon the harsh and scentless air,
Propose to the sick heart a stir
More subtle and a texture brighter
Than it has known or will encounter
In any earthly calendar;

The positive
Formed from this evil negative,
Shows what no year will ever give:
Spring's absolute.

Sang the angel in the tree:
pain prises the heart. See it stretch!
Narrow as the grave it was,
sang the leafy angel.

Fire in the marrow! sang
the angel in the tree,
pain pain on the inmost quick
another wave of it rises.

Pure pain taken
in the marrow the core the spirit's vein,
sang the birdy angel.
To your height it has added a cubit.

ALL SAINTS' DAY

Guedé Nimbo, it is your week.

The frangipani the flamboyant stir.
Flakes of sun in a ragged flight?
Yellow butterflies!

It does not look to me as though it were your week.

On the maupous' roots, the sisal fields, the cane—
(I can see for a hundred miles)—the Haitian sun,
presses its flame.

All Saints. All Souls. My dead are stirring too.
All souls, all saints. What of my dead,
Guedé Nimbo?

They stir in my blood in the cells of my brain in the sac
of my heart. And all my saints, my saints are gathering
in their silence.

It does not look like the week of the dead.

At home the leaves hush in the cold rain, the brittle
whisper of leaves hushes under the cold fine touch.
Death is evident.

The graywhite stones under the graywhite sky
are wet. The city of the dead within the city
gathers and waits.

The names the dates like a token a whisper full of nothing
but meaning; they invite the memory, that injured ghost;
memory is summoned.

Here there is no need for the dead to summon.

They are always here though the green verdant green, name,
    cape, valley
of green burns in the sun and the lizard—his black eye
set in turquoise—

shrunk from the giant past, like a toy jewel
flashes and stops, and the rose swags of bougainvillaea
glow; Guedé Nimbo

you are a stranger to me. But you are here.

Tonight while the cocks crow in the dark and the roped dogs
    hurl
themselves snarling, under thumbs, fingers, the blows of palms,
    the drums
your drums will drum

tonight, far from the raw clay of another country
I shall say in the dark *O holy Saints* . . . To those we have
    touched
death occurs.

On this one thing we can agree, Guedé Nimbo.

   11
In another country on another day the brittle bones whispered
    of pain
like leaves. Love touched the bones under the light dry skin and
    with its hand
shadowed the eyes.

The resolute heart beat beat; beat, drumming the difficult
    breath.
Deep in the eyes deep deep flicked knowledge and went out
    and came
a flick of answer.

It was night outside; outside there was wind.

The shadow of wings of the dark wings defined the lamp.

The heart beat beat; beat, the breath stirred the light bones in
    the lamp's
raw circle.

The little skull locked in its shell all secrets;
It was the heart's affair to beat, and so it did once more once
more; once more.

And then on an exact and delicate balance
something fled—on a sigh, the smallest sigh
under the very fingers.

Suddenly the heart beat hard once and the breath
raised the dead breast. This was mechanics this was nothing.
It was gone. The exact and delicate balance tipped.

One instant the treasure was there alive with mystery,
inestimable; unique, unique, unique. The next clock's tick
was to a thing.

Things are disposed of and this was disposed of:
the earth was breached again. All souls. All saints.
The city of the dead.

The clay was breached. All souls. All saints. *In those days
I heard a voice from heaven, saying to me, Write
Blessed are the dead.*

The intolerable clay was intolerably breached. *And all the angels
stood . . . for the familiar shape . . . and the ancients and the
     four
living creatures . . .*

All souls witness, all saints assist, the clay was breached . . .
    saying
Amen. Benediction and glory and wisdom and thanksgiving and
    honor
and power.

This was on another day in another country.

III
All souls. All saints—there is a turning in the air
a veil, like smoke of pearls, dissolves in the sun's flame.
Darkness is coming.

Your travesty I know: high hat, cigar, white shirt,
your skewed cross, faceless face; hungry and faceless saying
your syllable.

In the night hills Guedé Nimbo your drums will speak it: to-
    those-we-have—
touched, to those we have touched, to those we have *touched*
    death
occurs.

We have a quarrel but it is not this.

The colors go into dusk, the rose into rose, green into lime,
all into dusk: silent and fast the sky sucks them, darkness has
    them in its
dark filter.

In the blood in the cells of the brain in the sac of the heart
the knowledge of night filters the dark like smoke; intolerably
the sky is breached.

Cock and goat feel the dark, goat and cock feel how soon
the drums begin; Guedé Nimbo, Gue-dé Nim-bo
Gue-dé Nim-bo.

The heart beat, beat; beat, the breath stirred.

It was the heart's affair to beat and so it did:
In those days saying to me, Write . . . O holy saints. All souls.
All souls. All souls,

witness, all saints assist: the clay was breached.
The night is here. *Benediction and glory and wisdom*
in this dark

Honor neither hungry nor faceless. And, certainly, *power.*

He thought they were gone:
claw, horn, wing.
Not even a stir in the tree—
top monkey-swing.

An experienced hunter,
he knew quite well one starved thus.
But not the reason: Thirst's moonlit
Exodus?

He had on his blinders
and instead of his rifle, a sling—
(from day to day one never
knew about this part of the thing—)

when he saw the motion.
It would ripple and pass
untouched. Gazelle? Lion?
But there was game in the grass.

In the deeps, depths, sea's night of noon,
In the slow-motion silence and sliding slip
Of weed, wash, fish, in the night motion
Heavy with fathoms' lapses from the sun,
The diver in the black clasp of his ocean
Flares instantly, lit like a salty god,
In delirium. Breaks free as flame
From the pearl or plan or message of his mission;
May hand a shark his helmet, lose his name,
Cut the earth's cord . . .
   While far far far above,
Light lights the sea's blue pleasure—
Boat, sky, sun; the hissing swans of foam.
Love, love, these depths we seriously measure
All unprotected, the chart has showed
Unsounded. Yet so far our trove
Comes up, our blaze of treasure.

Inn Revisited

In the thin-lipped March matin
through the pane I had heat from spurious summer:
the geese yelled from yellow beaks and stepped
on splayed webs their soiled satin.

Up they rocked—(goose by one—)
like July, from the pond; all seven.
The black girl shook the sheets as with languor
from a surfeit of sun.

In hot green moved the seven
and the girl moved in tigerish light—
though raw trees were shaken and iron
had covered all heaven.

Now a white neat face
bends over the white sheets that palely tauten
hasty as winter work, though the print says July.
And the geese are no place.

Poet as Mute

for Hans Andersen

Meteor flying and the planets' chime
He, lying like another on mattress and pillow
Hears—as his ear as a shell rings hollow—
Knows—as water is known to the willow—
At midnight, on the turn and shift of time.

Anciently and again ensnared
By the treacherous offer of love and sleep,
Instead, the little mortal feels his shape
Inflated out of scale by savage hope,
Huge with the giant wonder of the word.

He went down to the sea-witch's domain
Wearing the little mermaid's mask:
Treasure washed to wrack and husk,
The ghost of riches distant from the moon.

By the dead seamaid polyps' hands have riven
In terror she passes (bright with bane
The gushing mud, the house of bone)
To sell a tongue for the far chance of heaven,

So that later, when questioned by the handsome prince
"she looked at him very mournfully from her dark
blue eyes, for" (we know) "she could not speak."
Not once upon a time, alas; not once . . .

Now as Eliza, speechless as she spins
(Against enchantment and the fagot

Of troubled king and fierce prelate)
Brothers and princes from the feathers of swans.

Silent in silence she, by graveyard stone
Where hideous the lamias gambol,
Spied on has plucked the stinging nettle
With the eleventh-hour-and-shirt unspun.

But though the great birds assemble in glory, the flame
Will have her, for the flax unfinished,
The shining proof of mail, unfurnished;
Always the youngest brother has the swan's shame.

There is no use expecting the penalty to be lighter,
Nor bells to ring themselves in carols
Nor fagots sprout shoots to spell out morals
In scarlet roses. That was elsewhere and later.

The fire climbs faster, the foam purls over the beach,
The foam purls over the sand, the flames flow faster:
See paradise's mute, the captive master.
Tongueless the seamaid, silent the swans' sister,
Silent our brother in the terrible silence of speech.

Paul, that friend and heir to Christ,
Fought the tiger and the sea.
By the bloody ghost of Stephen
And the stones that let him free,
Paul—with Peter, Mary, Dismas—
Pray for us in charity.

The Magdalene while it was dark
Came to the tomb and found it empty.
By the violent common noon
Of your shame's discovery
Mary—with Paul, Dismas, Peter—
Pray for us in charity.

Peter, crucifixion's clown,
Died with earth where sky should be.
By your tongue of faithless friend
Quicker than the cockerel's cry,
Peter—with Dismas, Mary, Paul—
Pray for us in charity.

Dismas leapt to paradise,
Straight from wood to God went he.
By your clever thievish hand
Later struck upon the tree,
Dismas—with Mary, Paul and Peter—
Pray for us in charity.

Mighty saints who purify
Zealot, traitor, whore and thief,
Peter, Dismas, Mary, Paul
Pray for us in charity.

Shibboleth

Tonight I saw the marred and frosted moon.
It sat high in the bare sky over
your naked shoulder and the thin rich line
of vineleaves in the green glass bottle.
And instantly here was the curve of the child's arm;
also the dying man drying in his corner
when the truck took the colored crests of bough
with shouts, in the strong autumn ether.
Child was in the bleachers, old man inside the window; bared
sky was around the moon which was frosted and marred.

Four years had shaped the arm to make its mythical curve
melt to the wrist like love:
the diamond blazed, the runner held,
but the fold of the curve drew down the word.
The old man dried in his chair behind glass
to hear them bear away
the colored tops-of-trees the linesmen's truck
shook in shimmers away down his October street.
To the moon's green vine came the trapped man's motionless
    form,
to the lovers' midnight came the curve of the arm.

The desperate Ephraimites cried "Sibboleth!" to the watch;
so cried, and died for the letter.
Now here is Gilead, but here and here your breath
says "Shibboleth"; so says the moony bottle and its vine;
so says the utter curve. But the boughs that vanish and the slow-
dying man drying by glass

say "Shibboleth!" All sibling angels of a password
heard in the midnight room at the point of love.
What angels? Tell me, what angels? The angels of death
and love, to the Gileadites crying "Shibboleth!"

Pitch Lake

*The underworld was beneath the earth's surface but above
the nether waters, the great abyss.*

Introduction to The Epic of Gilgamesh

Erishkigal, Ishtar's fresh sister, sky-
goddess, darkened to a queen of shadows,
she too a shade.
She never came back, unlike Persephone
released to gilded meadows
on the flowers' tide.

There are two motions here: Persephone's
and the sister's. The first led up
to the place known
and the face. The second, to where dust lies
on door and bolt, and hope drops.
That motion led down.

Through the Trinidad blaze no gaze can be trusted:
the pontooned truck seems motionless to our eyes
as we step warily where
like a desert but blueblack, heaved, crested,
now, here, the pitch lake lies
in noon's stare.

Actually it is sinking—but so smooth, so light,
so noiseless . . . the men who shine and bake
to load it know;
one will leap to loose the pitch grip at the right
last instant—the stirred stiff lake
will let it go.

But its skeleton sister was caught in the bubble
of black, in the shift of shiny suck.
Someone was late.
So the men did their best by expensive trouble;
knowing the law of gravity-in-luck,
they gutted the wraith.

It is half under, gradually grim.
But only insects or the smallest mice
go where it goes,
except for minnows that appear and swim
in tiny pools like fissures in black ice
that open. And then close.

But the other motion is up. Something constantly shoves
a shining black up to the day.
They hack and lift
but the dark level is constant, the asphalt moves
up, up, opens its way:
breach, rift.

At all costs, no symbols—one motion
is up. The other, down. This bright
black sets forth
what is familiar to passion or caution.
Fatally knowing, we step, lightly, to fixed earth.

The greedy angel with no eyes
carried off all each night, and the next morning
let memory mince up, with a pious smile bringing
facsimiles in painted cardboard.

In Seville
he lifted the whole weight of orangeblossom scent
and went off with it and spangled dolphins spouting crystal
and some cascade music frozen into tiles. At Arles
the curly cypress spiked with stars
chanted *Saint Vincent ora in your dark blaze pro nobis,* but
he covered it with his feathers and left
a picture-postcard in its place.

At Juan-les-Pins he took the trembling lights and gradually
the loud cries of the frogs—
(at Juan-les-Pins where the man said "frog sounds like a frog,
        but *grenouille* looks like a frog.")
At Almeria he made off with the Spanish Moroccans
who squealed over strange cards and gorged mint tea.

I could not forgive the loss of the wild doves
at Ronda from the holes in the cliffs nor the disappearance
of the oldest bull-ring while full of Roman and attentive ghosts.

By night, by dark, he stripped the senses, struggle or not,
and made off with all things in his plumy net:
he took the ferns, at Monserrate, and almost
the face of love. But that would not go
to sleep; or only as stars in water.

The Starfish

The great starfish was hauled up by a point.
Yellow and crimson with hard intricate bumps
it blazed wetly O it was regal and starry,
heavy cool cousin marine in the washy wave
a star a star.

But it was alive.

Its shape had a link with the steely stellar
steadfast light—no less than in ether
it conformed to its points of a star.

The sun strange as hot hell
attacked it in the grass. It could not
move. But it did. It
curled faintly

in the first sign of corruption—the distortion
of proportion,
of the correspondence between relative points. O a star
is not hap hazard, only sickened
to death;
so, two points went
off center and the middle warped lightly.

It was a race.
Would the ants
clean it before irreparable corruption?
To gut a star
is a job—the ants were overtaxed.

There is a technique in destruction-through-preservation of star-
     fish:
To pleasure the pink lady's project a
gentle black boy
placed
it on an anthill.

The ants worked, worked, small, shiny, quick.
They came too late; the
water's stellar space or the motion of space in the wave's wash
     or
the coral bed had corresponded to the nothing neighborhood
of a star.

Like a tide the light of color drew back, tide, tide
sucked by the wicked wick of sun:
the shape went even more off starshape.

The connection snapped.

Even before the ants finished
it had disappeared from the categories of desire

its silent cool marine starlife warm and warped
its starhood stung to chaos.

Here is your sting. O
death, where is your star?

Harlequin speaks by the moon's light:
By the light of the moon, Peter, my friend
Peter, from your dark window bend

(Dark and moon and shadow blend)
To listen at least. (The bare boughs soar,
Pencil the wild white snow—) lend

Me your cold gold pen to write
By the bright moon, Peter, my friend,
One word. One single word, no more.

The cold step of the hungry whore
Strikes on the stone, the cold stars bend
Over my small dead candle-end,

My naked hearth is dead tonight
I have no fire there to mend.
For God's love, open your door.

The fiddler crab fiddles, glides and dithers
dithers and glides, veers; the stilt-eyes
pop, the legs prance the body glides, stops,
the front legs paw the air like a stallion,
at a fast angle he veers fast, glides, stops,
dithers, paws.

The water is five shades of blue. On the rocks
of the reefridge the foam yelps leaping, the big rock
here is glutted with breathers under their clamped clasp,
scarab shapes and tiny white and black whorls.
The lacy wink lapses, behind it the black lustre
lapses and dulls.

I saw the fiddler crab veer, glide, prance
dither and paw, in elliptical rushes
skirt the white curve and flatten on the black
shine. He veered in a gliding rush
and up to piled sand and into a trembling hole
where grains fell past him.

I imitated him with my five fingers, but not well.
Nothing else moved on the sand. He came out.
My hand cast a shadow. He raised a notch and ran
in tippity panicky glide to the wave's wink.
Each entirely alone on his beach; but who
is the god of the crabs?

On the balcony over the rocks two hours later
The Spanish-Chinese boy brought him to show.

His stilted eyes popped over three broken legs
but he ran with the rest of them over the edge
and died on the point of the drop down
twenty feet.

So it is simpl.: he can be hurt
and then he can die. In all his motions
and marine manoeuvres it was easy to miss
on the sand how I should know him and he me
and what subject matter we have in common.
It is our god.

A passing fiend caught him changing from reader to writer.
First he was happy on a heath, or in a dark wood, was it?
Then jekyll-to-hyde, and the ardent successful reader
Gone. And what was there, the fiend knew exactly.

"You had something in mind to tell us?" the fiend said softly.
It watched him with amusement, stirring its wings.
He could only say, "I looked up and something happened to
    that yellow iris."
"Something unique?" said the fiend, deadly sympathetic.

In its barbarous feathers, "Anon," said the fiend.
Rapidly it added, "Blake and Chaucer, Dante. And Euripides."
But before it found an F, he had said again,
Hopeless but helpless, "Something happened to the iris."

"Pride," said the fiend, casting up its eyebrows.
All its feathers shimmered. It raised a claw and said
"Goethe; Holderlin . . ." (here he lost track, thinking
Of the poems in Sanskrit, Greek and Persian) ". . . Marlowe,"
    it was saying,

"Nerval, Ovid, Pushkin." (Pause.) "Quasimodo . . ."
He could see the iris suck its secret deeper.
"Racine," said the fiend from its snaky feathers,
"Shak-" here he flung a stone, which went through the fiend.

What had touched the iris, gone into, come out of,
Now he had no notion. All was still as shock.

Fiend went into feathers, feathers into fiend.
"Gentle fiend, come back! Take the yellow iris!"

But no one knew—not Tasso, Ungaretti, Verlaine,
Not one knew what had happened to the iris;
He, on earth, in planets, galaxies, anywhere—
Only he, only he, only he must say.

I. LOOKING DOWN, AT DELPHI

Suddenly the oracle gives me my answer—
delphic, naturally. Up
the mountain, on a dwarf
donkey, an old fat man with three
dogs—white dog,
black dog, small black dog with three
legs—rises. All three
dogs run up
the cold early mountain dark in dark mist; but the small
black dog, though bounding, bounds behind.
Stonecold mist, but from daisies
orange and yellow about
the small hooves stepping
the sun shines up.

II. THE SPARROWS AT DELPHI

Sparrows
are in the Treasury of Athens, in the holes
between the pale honey-veined blocks;
the sparrows are whole
and have not been
restored.
Not even a beak or a wing-tip is
chipped.
To the hollow spaces of the empty Athe-
nian Treasury
on the god's slope at Delphi
go in the sparrows.

The fish had leaped and leaped and leaped in the motion
of terror and down where the shadow of a shade
was lost it swam. There he sent word and emotion.
They foundered. When he raised his hand to shade
against the razzle-dazzle sea, the motion
cast on his wooden world a hand of shade.

In three bright leaps it had recomposed its sea.
It was alone: in that universe it would
meet nothing else nothing nothing. The sea
held not one other thing, nothing. The sea would
keep up and out his ship. He need not turn to see
behind him his masted world: vibration, words, and caulked
     wood.

In a cold wreck and wrack it spawned to swell
its trillion trillion, the salt sexual sea. That fish
was its only thing alive. In the long salt fertile swell
moved one alive. Felt itself swim, that fish,
mated with itself, ate itself. Swill and swell
deep debris sunstruck slant: "I" said that fish.

The spraysoaked beadbright teak of the rail of the ship
moved down and up, he rode his planks to stare
down through the glare glaze. "Worship," he said, "friendship."
Where the fish had gone with its silver and round stare
and universe of one, he tried to go; but the ship
stayed on top and the fish's sea refracted his stare.

In the blue, turquoise, black depth, in the glide dart and turn
that fish one cruised with downdrawn fishmouth saying "I"
forever and forever. Ship sails, sun shines, moon turns
all tides, but that ravenous mouth unshuttered eye
goes alone round the sun round the moon round the sea, turns,
eternal turner, alone says only "I".

Some time away from the sea but still with salt
in his blood that keeps a tide, in the water
of his most bitter tears, some time away from the salt
swell that got him, he sees that fish under its tons of water
one thing in the ocean. Now he feeling the spray's salt
on his skin, says "you" into the wind over the water.

Florida rang with rain the eve of Christ's mass; the gallinules
     trod lily-pads,
Anhinga herons hung the boughs like fruit, the willows shud-
     dered ghosts of moony egrets.

Rain fell on dolphins' plunge and curve and secret smile
in sea and air torrent; the turquoise Gulf black met Christ's
     birthnight.

The rain rained on the keys—Key Largo, Saddlebunch, Knight's
     Key and Crawl.
Seven Mile Bridge billowed with rain, Gulf, bridge and Ocean
     jumped with rain on Christmas eve. The ducks

rocked sleeping on the small cold waves and Christmas fell
     upon their feathers.
In the Everglades the alligator sailed with half a grin and
     Christmas pelted on his midnight scales.

The roadside canals swelled, eddied, boiled; herons that step
     and peer
slept dripping; the rushes
rattled and rushed and the palms tore their hair;
the surf roared and the palms roared like the water, the water
     rained like palm-fronds on the sea.

The sea-grapes spun with water; the sand silently took God's
     rain,
Christmas fell on the swamp, on Okeechobee, inside the jungle
     raindrop;

the thick anonymous green grew into Christmas,
the jungle staggered, singing;
upon the mangroves came the son of man.

The drops sprang back from lily-pads, rain rang the land like
    chimes:
the baby came at midnight to the rushes.

Fire wakes with a burst in the tower of leaf—
(Leaves and fire are ever the dead and the quick,)
Distorted, like flies in death—(they were flexible, green,)
Leaves go on the lizard-tongues that leap and lick.

But being an element, fire will not change,
It harbors another thing on which it has fed.
The bodies fly up: the host which went by the flame,
Each terrified body crowned by its sentient head.

As praise to the teakwood profile, the cold stone mouth,
Out of old nights, in jungle, on temple-altar;
As medicinal scourge to the wilful ailing soul
While parchment pardon was raised, should the devil falter;

The Parsee widow, fifteen, and enamoured of breath;
The crone who kept only one cow, but whose eye could be-
        witch;
The man of our nation and day, in the piney growth,
We threw back as he crept from the core of the burning pitch.

In the gust of the April flames see how they blow;
Their voices lift, up streams their forking hair . . .
Rake the innocent leaves, pile the pure brush. You invoke
Fire unchanged. Always its host is there.

The Danish mobile has a puffed gilt star
that swings just slightly in the slightest air
that swings just slightly four attendants
mobile in rose bell-bottomed skirts on a lower level.

The angels stir in the small perturbation of the air
careening slowly, and the star, leveling,
slowly careens. Early the shafted angels
sheer the sun; but in total darkness too the mobile levels.

Wires rig the star, wires rig the heads of the angels
my friend suspended in the crowded invisible air.
Atoms collide, ash slips, and death elects. Meanwhile
careens (yet level) the counterpoint of love, the Danish mobile.

Cul de Sac

Cul de Sac

Cul de Sac

In the grassplot's center was a bed of red roses,
A circle in a pear; round-eyed and fragrant
The great tame blossoms loaded the noon
With pleasure; the grass sparkled under the sprinkler;
The trees ranked black, banking the driveway;
The ferns sprang, still. A treetrunk came alive

With a cautious coon face cocked round the bole.
It watched the brightness and Erlend
Who held his hoe in wonder: Enemy
Watched watching enemy. Sidelong
The raccoon in silence without fear or cunning
Came down and shambled into the sun.

Out of the woods and the shade and the silence
It crept toward the sunny boy on the grass
Gaudy with drops. It crouched and lifted
Anxious and silent in the blaze
Of sun and water and roses—its head
To what it should have known to be deadly.

Erlend got food in a white cracked bowl.
The raccoon ate it, using his hands,
His sinewy fingers; but he would not drink.
He wove over to Erlend's feet and stared.
His eyes stared up, dark from the dark fur,
He stared up in silence but urgently.

The rest was ugly and rapid. He was mad.
He stiffened, upright, water came from his mouth,
His mask contorted and he fell; got up;
Reared stiff, and fell, got up, and ran
Around. Shots ended the dumb-show suffering,
The raccoon was quiet in a bloody ruff.

It was insanity that brought him
Silent from the normal wood's hostility
Onto the bright unnatural grassplot,
Pigeon-toed, shambling, aping a pet;
But he was neither sane nor degraded;
He came from shadows to the blazing day.

He came to the devil-angels of his myth,
Crept to the glare of danger to be saved;
Alone, a crazy alien in the trees,
Was drawn to break bread in a travesty
Of friendship. The calendar and woods forgot him.
Not so the human who succored and shot him.

I passed between the bell and the glass
window. Santa rang his bell. The wax girl leaned
forward: she was naked and had red nails.
Santa wore spectacles and rang his bell.
The second-floor trees raised rainbows in the dusk.

The snow fell lightly. I did not stop to ask
the scarlet man a favor; the girl leaned as if to give
from her wax body blood or heat or love.
But she was wax. Her belly and breasts were shaped;
she wore black pumps and leaned, above the pavement.

The unique snowflake died on the cement.
I passed between her wax eyes and his clapper.
The steelrimmed eyes watched me, the wax eyes watched the
    watcher.
He rang, she leaned, to give me my message: that I must breed
alive unique love from her wax and his steel.

This wind blows still in stone; blows
in still stone: this
stonestill wind lifts

the draped folds, rocks
the wing-tip, combs
back the stonecold curls.

The body breasts it, blown
almost back: the breasts are shaped
by the wind's touch: the breasts' breath

drinks it salt and fresh; in
the instant of centuries that salt
seawind bright

with invisibility, blows back
the fluent tender folds: watch
it tense the instep,

rush the neck's thrust. See:
it plows the stone like fluid wheat
in its passage.

The sky stainless, flawed by one gull
And stretched across no sight, silk-tight;
Salt noon stranded like a hull
In clearest light;

Clarity of palms splits the sun
To strike and shiver on the blue blue view,
So perfection not ended nor begun
is perfectly true.

The hollow setting (while the jewel lags),
Infinite, unsoiled, smiling, clear:
          Appear!
Sly, dirty, cruel, lost and in rags
The beloved is here.

On that hot journey I became aware of water.
At Panajachel the water ran in the strawberry gardens.
Through the dusty hedge, from the path's deep dust, I could
    hear water:
it was low-voiced and bright from the hot pipes; and the fingers
    of the pickers
were wet and stained and shiny with water and juice;
the small brown girls in red squatted and picked
to this sound, of water that gratified the red warm bumpy cones.

At the end of the puffs of dust, at the floor of the dust path,
Atitlán: deep, blue; at levels tepid, cool, chill, cold
below the volcanic perfect cone and its tethered cloud;
all morning it mirrored the cone and the cloud,
the wind boiled it after that in cones of its own
hurrying it over drowned Indians, a priest, and older things
in a secret heap at a depth it has so far not disclosed.

At Acolman the cistern in the center of the courtyard
of the roofless convent held all that blurred in the day's breath—
what could stir stone and figures of pain and grace but water?
At Morelia the children and fountains jumped, the zocolo's
    blown fountains
sprayed the children, the children and fountains played.
But this was the merest blandest brush with water,
its stage-effects palmed off on the uninitiate.

I drove through days of a desert blind and cracked and white
    with light
and stones, bones, bone stones and limbs of barebone trees;

there were doves, vultures, coyotes; thorns, iguanas, doves,
and the shadows were stunted; the goats traveled in haloes
of dust and slipped on the stones of furnace arroyas.
Once a dusty pair of coyotes leaped down
into a rocky gully and raised a little yellow cloud that floated.

The dusty doves and the muscle-bound vultures rocking
like wrestlers over the split earth toward their feast were
clouded, and everything was silent and yellow with that ghost
    of earth:
the sky shone through its haze; the dazed earth gave no dew.
Water was before the eye, in the mind, the ear, the bone,
before the parched lips, on the parched tongue.
All that land hummed like a wire with absent water.

It was sudden.
That slightly heaving hotel, from a folder,
was there one instant: through the glass a bloodorange ball
just diving, a pure blue desert of dusk
on the other horizon; a motion, the symbol of seas;
music, and drinks, and the self-conscious apparel,
the relative facets, of steward and poster, and sun-disc
just hidden.

The ship spoke
with a minotaur sound from around and under
and we raised our eyes: but the sea was gone:
sub-sun, the peel of moon, the plausible shift
of dunes of water, our precious image of movement—
gone, gone, clean gone. The fog was at the pane.
No shore behind us; ahead in the breathy drift
no port.

Supported
by shore and port, now we had neither.
There was only here. The ship was here
in the fog. The ship roared and the fog blotted
us into itself and whirled into its rifts,
and the sealess skyless fear—and there was fear—
had nothing to do with sinking—at least, not
into water.

Worse:
when we went below, at the familiar turn

a bulkhead reared instead, metal and huge—
and trapped, we turned from that hulk and hastened
through stranger stairs and came from a different angle
to a cabin stiller and smaller though none of its objects had
    moved.
But the mirror stirred like fog when we looked for the fastened
    face.

We crept
through fog all night but it closed behind us:
around and very close above:
Only below in the black the self-lit fishes
passed ignorantly among the racks of wrecks
and all the water held its tongue and gave
no password; and so sealed in our motionless passage
we slept.

The bell
for the bulkhead doors to open, woke us.
Everything had been reconnected: sun to the sea,
ship to the sun, smiles to our lips, and our names related
to our eyes. Who could—in that brassy blue—
have stillness to harbour the memory
of being relative to nothing; isolated;
responsible?

The reindeer
fastened to the great round eye
that glares along the
Finnish forest track
runs runs runs runs runs
before that blast of light, will die
but not look back

will not
look back, or aside, or swerve
into the black tall deep
good dark of the forests of winter
runs runs runs runs runs
from that light that thrust through his brain's nerve
its whitehot splinter.

The reindeer
has all the forests of Finland to flee
into, its snowy crows and owlly
hush; but over the icy ties
runs runs runs runs runs
from his white round i-
dée fixe until he dies.

To his west
is wide-as-the-moon, to his right
is deep-as-the-dark, but
lockt to his roaring light
runs runs runs runs runs

(110

the fleeing flagging reindeer
from, into, the cold
                    wheels'
                         night.

Almost nothing concerns me but communication.
How strange: Up the Orinoco, once, far
up the Orinoco after jungle miles, great flowerheads
looping the treecrests, log-crocodiles, crocodile-logs, bob-haired
Indians naked in praus: a small, hot, town and in an upper din-
     ing-room
plashed at by a fountain, cooled by fans, guardian of a menu
     the size of a baby,
speaking six languages, with seven capital cities behind his eyes,
     a headwaiter,
a man, who said without hope, "*And when does your ship sail?*"
     And no one
said to him, "*What are you doing here?*"

In the hall of the inn at Mont Serrat I came out of my room
     and
"*Stand back, stand back!*" cried the criada in her softest Span-
     ish, "*the bride—*
the bride is coming!" out of her room, down the hall, down to
     the steps
on her way to the church, to the groom. She was pale, and dark;
     she clouded
the carpet with the mist of her train, she moved by me but
     turned and bent and caught
my fingerbones seeing me like fate, watching the three of her
     the old, tall, childhood girl,
the darkly seen half-a-thing, and the white bride lost on the
     point of love, and "*Buenas,*

o buenas tardes!" she called into my ear, she crushed my fingers
    and laughed with panic
into my widened eyes and went proudly on whispering
over the hall runner.

I drove five madwomen down a roaring redhot turnpike in a
    July
noon; the one behind me had a fur ragged coat gathered about
    her in that furnace;
she reached in the horrid insides of a purse and offered me a
    chocolate, liquid
and appalling. "*Look! Look! A bird!*" I cried and flung it over
    the side
and munched my empty jaws as she turned back, and cried:
    "*How good!*"
And while the others hummed and cursed, and watched simply,
    suddenly she put
her lips—behind me—to my ear and soft as liquid chocolate
    came purling
the obscene abuse. "*Hush, hush, Laura, hush,*" said the nurse;
    "*the nice lady
likes you!*" Laura did not believe so, and went on softly, slowly,
    lovingly,
with O such misery of hate.

In frosty Philadelphia the freighter lay and loaded in the Sunday
ice. The great cranes swung, the huge nets grabbed and every-
    thing echoed from cold:

docks, warehouses, freightrails, ships' prows; everything clicked
    and echoed;
but it was possible to go down the long cold docks over the
    strange dark street under
the dim sky into a cold great warehouse Sunday still, up still
    cold stairs, along
a dark dim cold thin hall through a brown door into a small
    square room with lit
peaky candles and kneeling take—cool, slick, thin, little larger
    than a quarter—
God's blood and body charged with its speech.